j808.1
C428oW

T H A N K S G I V I N G
DETROIT PUBLIC LIBRARY

Knapp Branch Library
13330 Conant
Detroit, MI 48212

DATE DUE

NOV 26 1995
NOV 25 1996

DEC 0 2 1996

NOV 2 2 1997

APR   1994

Over the River and Through the Wood

Over the River and Through the Wood

by **Lydia Maria Child**

pictures by **Nadine Bernard Westcott**

HarperCollins*Publishers*

Over the river and through the wood,
To grandfather's house we go;

The horse knows the way
To carry the sleigh
Through the white and drifted snow.

Over the river and through the wood—
　Oh, how the wind does blow!
　　It stings the toes
　　And bites the nose,
　As over the ground we go.

Over the river and through the wood,
To have a first-rate play.
Hear the bells ring,
Ting-a-ling-ding!
Hurrah for Thanksgiving Day!

Over the river and through the wood,
Trot fast, my dapple-gray!
Spring over the ground
Like a hunting-hound!
For this is Thanksgiving Day!

Over the river and through the wood,
And straight through the barnyard gate.
We seem to go
Extremely slow—
It is so hard to wait!

Over the river and through the wood—
Now grandmother's cap I spy!

Hurrah for the fun!

Is the pudding done?
Hurrah for the pumpkin-pie!

Over the River and Through the Wood

With galloping motion

arr. Ray Kimmelman

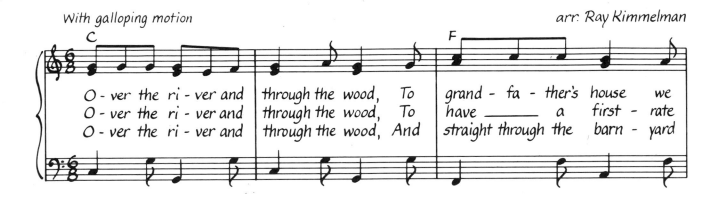

O - ver the ri - ver and through the wood, To grand - fa - ther's house we
O - ver the ri - ver and through the wood, To have _____ a first - rate
O - ver the ri - ver and through the wood, And straight through the barn - yard

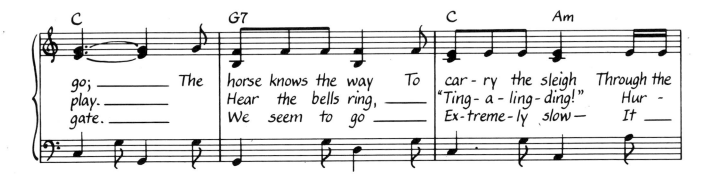

go; _____ The horse knows the way To car - ry the sleigh Through the
play. _____ Hear the bells ring, _____ "Ting- a - ling- ding!" Hur -
gate. _____ We seem to go _____ Ex- treme- ly slow— It _____

D7 ... *G7* ... *C*

white ___ and drift - ed snow. ____ | O-ver the ri-ver and | through the wood— Oh,
rah for Thanks-giv - ing Day! ____ | O-ver the ri-ver and | through the wood, Trot
is ___ so hard to wait! ____ | O-ver the ri-ver and | through the wood— Now

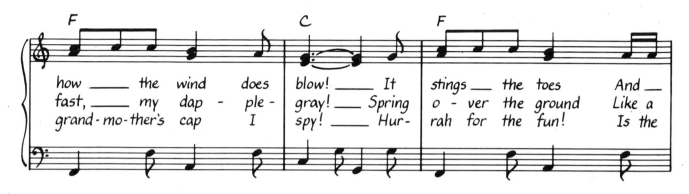

F ... *C* ... *F*

how ___ the wind does | blow! ____ It | stings ___ the toes And ___
fast, ___ my dap - ple - | gray! ___ Spring | o - ver the ground Like a
grand - mo-ther's cap I | spy! ____ Hur- | rah for the fun! Is the

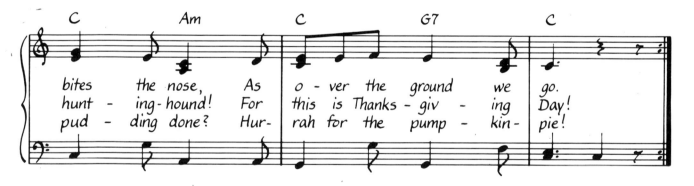

C ... *Am* ... *C* ... *G7* ... *C*

bites the nose, As | o - ver the ground we | go.
hunt - ing-hound! For | this is Thanks - giv - ing | Day!
pud - ding done? Hur- | rah for the pump - kin- | pie!

For Jenny R.

The poem "Over the River and Through the Wood" was originally
titled "A Boy's Thanksgiving Day," published in 1844 in
Flowers for Children by Lydia Maria Child.

Over the River and Through the Wood
Text by Lydia Maria Child
Illustrations copyright © 1993 by Nadine Bernard Westcott
Printed in the U.S.A. All rights reserved.
Music copying and caligraphy by Christina T. Davidson
Typography by Michele Chism
1 2 3 4 5 6 7 8 9 10 ❖
First Edition

Library of Congress Cataloging-in-Publication Data
Child, Lydia Maria Francis, 1802–1880.
  [Boy's Thanksgiving Day]
  Over the river and through the wood / by Lydia Maria Child ; pictures by
Nadine Bernard Westcott.
    p.   cm.
  Summary: An illustrated version of the well-known text describing the
joys of a Thanksgiving visit to grandmother's house.
  ISBN 0-06-021303-5. — ISBN 0-06-021304-3 (lib. bdg.)
  1. Children's songs—Texts. [1. Thanksgiving Day—Songs and music.
2. Songs.] I. Westcott, Nadine Bernard, ill. II. Title.
PZ8.3.C4335Ov 1992   92-14979
782.4216'0268—dc20   CIP
                                                                       AC